TABLE OF CONTENTS

D1707220

HARDCORE RESOURCES

Facebook
125,000 followers
Fan: https://www.facebook.com/HardcoreCloser/
Group: https://www.facebook.com/groups/salestalk/
Personal:
https://www.facebook.com/realryanstewman

Twitter
10,000 followers
Personal: https://twitter.com/ryanstewman
Business: https://twitter.com/hardcorecloser

LinkedIn
6,000 followers
Personal: https://www.linkedin.com/in/ryanstewman
Business: http://www.linkedin.com/co/hardcorecloser

Instagram
20,000 followers
Personal: https://www.instagram.com/ryanstewman/
Business:
https://www.instagram.com/hardcorecloser/

#43 Business Podcast on iTunes, 3,000 subscribers
https://itunes.apple.com/us/podcast/ the-hardcore-closer-podcast/id1098856846?mt=2

YouTube
1.5 million views
https://www.youtube.com/user/ryanstewman

Clyxo
www.Clyxo.com/Closer

Snapchat
ryanstewman

Skype
ryanstewman

Blog
400,000 Visitors Monthly
Sales Talk For Sales Pros
www.HardcoreCloser.com
Articles, Digital Products, Training Resources

Books

- *Bulletproof Business: Protect Yourself Against The Competition (2016)*
- *Kick Ass - Take Names, Emails and Phone Numbers (2015)*
- *Hardcore [c]loser,* ***A Top Business Book of all time, Amazon (Best Seller)*** *(2015)*

PART ONE

HOW TO KICK ASS

These days, business is all about accessibility in a world where everyone has the internet 24/7 in the palm of their hand. People want instant access to the people who pull the trigger and make decisions. This includes social media, video, email, phone, tech, chat and any other platform. If you are not utilizing every communication device available to make sales, promote your product, show your amount of services and perform customer service, then you are missing out on business in two ways: business you could have had, and business you risk losing to competition.

To begin with, I suggest you invite everyone to your personal Facebook profile. Make that your hub. Over a billion people are now on Facebook. Everybody you know has a Facebook account, whether they admit to logging into it frequently or not. Trust me, the numbers don't lie. Facebook has become the ultimate communication device. You can call somebody. It has a phone feature you to access, you can chat, send text messages and emails, join groups and pods, like pages, add comments and post to your own wall or others. Through Facebook, virtually everything and every way you can think of to make contact with others exists. I even run a kick ass sales group on FB called Sales Talk With Sales Pros that's filled with serious savages. Every time any new way of communication comes across Facebook, Facebook buys it and incorporates it within the system, or they just build their own systems. They bought Instagram. They've purchased all these other applications that have allowed them to have this awesome platform of communication. The way of the future is to use Facebook as your contact management database. You are going to have to use your personal profile, unless you want to pay serious money to play though, which we will talk about later.

I know what's happening right now. People reading this book, are saying, "But Ryan, I don't want to be friends with people on my personal profile. I have a business page for that. I created another profile for that. It's all bullshit." If you're having to fake who you are in today's society, it's fucking bullshit. If you have to pretend you're one way on one profile, only to be your real self on another profile, you're sending mixed signals to the Internet, the universe and those around you. You're confusing yourself, too, whether you realize it or not. You're living two lives online.

You may say, "Well, I drink." So? It's legal, last time I checked. "But, I go out and party with my single girlfriends, or my single guy friends, or my married girlfriends, or my married guy friends." That's something most everybody does from time-to-time, or on the weekends, during the week, or even seven days a week. Whatever. I live in America. I don't know where you're reading this book, but for those of us who live here, I know we can do whatever the hell we want to when it comes to going out. A good rule of thumb for you to consider: if you are embarrassed about something you're doing and you wouldn't put it online, you probably shouldn't do that shit. I'm just saying. I'm not telling you to live in a glass house, but I do.

Maybe it's your first time to ever be exposed to anything I've got to say. So, let me share with you, my background.

When I talk about what it takes to kick ass, I mean it from the heart. When I talk about what it takes to succeed, as you read this book, you'll realize that I mean it and that I have done it. I live in a glass house and have nothing to hide. I've been married and divorced three times. I've been bankrupt once, adopted and even gone through foreclosure. I've also been in prison twice and in jail numerous times. I've had several speeding tickets and several slaps on the wrist. I've had my house raided. I've had my apartment raided. I've been pulled over for no damn reason and arrested when I should have been let go. I've also been pulled over for things I should've gotten in trouble for, only to walk. I'm not scared to sit here and tell you all of that.

That's a heavy load I just dropped on you. Think about it. I don't have a funky story about how one time I did drugs or something similar to relate with you. I just told you a dozen or so things that have gone completely wrong in my life. These are things that would cause most people to quit, yet I continue to kick ass. I'm going to teach you why. I don't want you to take what I just said lightly. I've said it so many times at this point I tend to skip over it when I talk about it or write about it. Let me go into a little bit of detail with you.

When I was five or six years old, I started to notice my parents fought a lot. I noticed they would fight more than my friends' parents. At the age of six or seven—I don't remember how old I was exactly—my birth father and mother split up. While my father went on to do his thing, my mother moved on, met a guy, married him and he became my stepfather. When my birth father got behind on child support, my stepfather offered to adopt me to erase the child support my father owed. I agreed to it even though it was a weird situation. My name went from being Ryan Russell McCord to legally becoming Ryan Keith Stewman, who I am known as today. When I went to school afterwards, I had to explain to all the kids why I had a different name and a different dad. They wanted to know what was going on. In a really small town, it was awkward. Shortly after that, we moved out of the town. I'm not sure if my parents did it as a favor to me, or for themselves. But we moved back about a year later.

I've always been a troubled kid. My first day of kindergarten, the principal pulled me in her office and spanked my ass. I couldn't tell you what for, but it sent me on a long journey towards hating institutions and authority. As a young man, I was adopted, and then made fun of at school. I felt like I sometimes had to fight. I remember getting my ass whipped by the principal and getting my ass whipped by other kids. There were also times I whipped their asses. I grew up rough and hated going to school.

I couldn't throw a football, couldn't hit a golf ball and couldn't shoot a basketball. My parents would tell me things like, "Son, you're really good at sports. You played on the championship team." I was like, "Mom, I was eight years old. It was Little League. That shit doesn't count." While those guys kept growing and getting better at throwing a football, I started slowing down. I knew I had to do something besides try to play sports.
I had so much tension built up inside of me, my adopted father could see it. It caused a lot of friction between us.

Sometimes the friction reached a point where he was so angry, he would hit me. I worked for him at a car wash. I had worked there since I was about eight years old. By the time I was 13 or 14, I started selling car washes. When a customer came in and wanted a $10 wash, it was my job to up-sell them into a $14 to $18 wash. I would practice and got very good at it and I made a commission from the sales. I enjoyed sales so much that at 17 years old, I left school to sell car washes full time. I was making about $400 to $600 a week. Which, back then, was decent money, especially for a 16 or 17-year old kid. I made the choice to leave school because the principal and I got into an argument over earrings. He was willing to sacrifice my education over a pair of earrings. Goddamn control freaks and hard-headed kids. Regardless, I left school and embarked on a journey of my own.

My father and I continued to get in big fights that sometimes came to blows. One of his friends was sleeping with my girlfriend. Creepy situation, right? The guy was another manager for the car wash. When I found out, I kicked rocks, left home and lived on the streets for a few months. I went to jail for little shit like speeding tickets that I couldn't afford to pay, but I mostly slept on friends' couches. I just needed a place to lay my head and a place to take a shower. I worked odd jobs like painting houses, doing construction and electrical work and selling car washes at other places.

But I really didn't like manual labor. A) I wasn't that good at it; B) I wasn't heart and soul into it; C) it didn't pay worth a fuck. I also knew I had more talent than that type of work requires. I knew the people around me knew I had more talent because they always fucking picked on me. That's usually a sure sign someone knows you got something within you, when they try to repress it. Boy, was I picked on. I'm a man, I can take it. So, I continued to kick ass any way I could.

One day, I lost my job as an electrician and didn't know what to do. I had made some connections and sold a little weed from time to time. I did this in order to support my habit, because I do like to smoke weed. I still do to this day, in fact. I went to a guy and asked him, "Do you have anything stronger I can sell to make more money?" He suggested cocaine. I had never really messed with cocaine. I'd seen it a few times, but I had never used it. Regardless, I sold it for a few months and paid my rent. When I say I was selling cocaine, I'm not talking about kilos, and motherfucking pimps, gangsters and drug dealers. I'd go get an ounce, half ounce, sometimes two ounces of cocaine, which is about $1,000, and I would turn it into about $1,500. Then I would keep the extra after I paid my rent. I would do that once a week, maybe once every two weeks. It wasn't like I was making some huge amount of money. I was probably making the same money selling drugs that I was working at the car wash. I was just obviously having a better time.

I wasn't using it. I smoked weed like a fucking chimney, but I didn't do cocaine. My third ex-wife, who was my girlfriend back then, was totally against it. It's always good to have a woman to keep a guy in check. But one night, she broke up with me and disappeared to Oklahoma. It would be the day that forever changed my life.

Now, just to make things clear, when she left, I deserved it. A few nights before, I had taken her car keys and thrown them down a gutter to keep her from leaving. Desperate times call for desperate measures.

Luckily, this punk motherfucker who was my roommate at the time, dug them out of the gutter for her and allowed her to leave. Lucky for her, but unlucky for me. I didn't want her to leave because I knew she wasn't coming back. Back then, we used beepers. I beeped her and beeped her with my code: 404. She never hit me back.

So, my roommate and I decided to invite some girls over. They liked coke. I was drunk and smoking weed when they talked me into doing the coke, too. I was like *fuck* it. I didn't have my ex there to tell me not to do it. It's not her fault, but I had no bars and nobody holding me back from feeling pressured. Instead they were offering me a really good time, sex and everything else. So, I tried cocaine.

Now, don't get me wrong, I had tried coke one time when I was fifteen. That time I'd actually lied and said I had a problem with it so I could go to rehab and my parents would feel better about it. The coke I'd tried back then was safe, because it was chalk. I even told the guy, "Hey, man! This shit's not real."

I never really messed with it again until I was nineteen. On January 19, 1999 (lots of 9's in there), I did it. When I walked into the bedroom to get laid, I took my belt off and I don't remember anything after that. According to the report from the police, I had a seizure and died. The girl who was in the room with me, who also happened to be a stripper, hooker, prostitute, or whatever the hell, called 911 from our home phone. The police showed up at the front door. My roommate told them nothing was going on, but then she started screaming in the background, "There's a guy having a seizure in here!" The police came in the house, because at this point they've got probable cause. In my room, I had a safe with $150 worth of coke in it, baggies and scales. I also had an UZI. I believe a MAC-11 is the correct term for it.Regardless, I had a semi-automatic they found in the drawer. I don't even know where the hell I'd gotten it from. They took me to the hospital and arrested me.

I had made a series of bad decisions and now I was suffering the consequences, including death. If they brought me back to life, I was going to face charges from the state, and possibly, federal charges. I was probably going to prison for a long time.

Obviously, they did revive me. I woke up and discovered I was handcuffed to the bed in the hospital. The police officer heard the rattling of the handcuffs, came around the corner and said, "Ah, you're awake. You have the right to remain silent. Anything you say can and will be used against you in a court of law. You have the right to an attorney..." and whatever the fuck the rest of the Miranda Rights are. I asked them what I was being arrested for and he said, "Well, you gave us a fake name." Apparently, I had told them my name was Ryan Russell McCord at some point. "You had a gun and you had drugs. You're under arrest for manufacturing and delivering cocaine."

They didn't charge me for the gun. Or maybe they did and eventually dropped the charges. Soon, they'd actually let me out of jail with no bond because they wanted me to snitch. They showed me pictures. They had been following me for the last three days and I didn't know it, because I was naive. I got so fucking scared I told them I had no idea who the person in the picture was that they shoved in front of me. After that, they made me turn myself in and bond out.

I've always been a man. If I made a mistake, there was, and is no reason for me to put my mistakes off on somebody else. So, I manned up and bonded myself out. My bond was $25,000, which I didn't have. Remember, I'm selling drugs for two grand a month profit. I had to borrow money from my grandmother, my parents and their bosses. It was a sad situation. Then I had to get a lawyer. I had used one guy twice even though I'd realized he was just a shady punk. I used him again anyway because he's a lawyer and I needed him. But I don't like shady punks who live to get in people's back pockets, so I won't say his fucking name. Asshole! Regardless, we went through this two-year long process. It was January 19, 1999 when I got arrested. In November 2000, they finally sentenced me.

They offered me 20 years' probation. I told them, "I'm not even 20 years old." Then they offered me 10 years' probation, with it on my record, or 20 years without it going on my record. I couldn't agree to that. Next, they offered five years in prison. I begged for my life at that point. So, they made an exception to the rule and offered me two years in a Texas penitentiary. My lawyer told me, "Hey man, if you take the two-year gig, you'll do three months here in the county jail, which isn't a bad facility. It's very safe and very clean. You'll never even see Texas Department of Corrections or Criminal Justice. You'll make parole right here, since it's a first-time offense." Of course, I signed on it and went to jail. My grandparents were there. My parents were there. It was a sad day. Before that,

I'd had long hair, but I had shaved my head the day before. I had to look nice and presentable in court. Then they took me to jail.

About a week or two later, I heard a banging outside my cell. Boom! Boom! Boom! "Stewman, you're up. You're on the chain." Two weeks into my sentence and they were sending me to the Texas Department of Criminal Justice. My lawyer had lied to me to get me to sign the papers, so he could get the case off his caseload. I didn't want to go to prison. Nobody wants to go to prison. I especially didn't want to go to these prisons.

In prison, I got into fights. Sometimes, I got lucky with the bosses. When that happened, then I would have to deal with inmates, who resented me. For example, at one place I drove a tractor three days after arriving. I didn't know the rules. I'd never been to prison before. Some people had been waiting 20 years on this fucking farm to drive the tractor. For some reason they liked me. Maybe they thought I had skills or I worked hard. Anyway, they let me drive a tractor and it pissed a lot of people off. I had to take a ton of fucking punches to the face and give a ton of punches to the face as a consequence. Which, ultimately, moved me away from the facility. That's the kind of shit I went through. I experienced hate, in the House of Hate, as we called one of the units. I experienced gang fights, violence, everything you could imagine. I was also in some places that were mellow prisons. Over the course of about fifteen months, I saw five different prisons. Some were in downtown metropolitan areas. Some were out in the middle of nowhere. You'd be surprised where they hide prisons among you.

I got to see a side of Texas I'd never seen before. I'll never forget the first day I got off that bus. One inmate was crippled and in a wheelchair. They kicked him off the bus and made him drag himself by his elbows through the rain into the entrance. Told him, "Wheelchairs are for pussies, and there ain't no pussy in a men's penitentiary." Pretty powerful stuff to make a first impression on a young man who was barely 20 years old.

I went through a lot of rough times until I finally got released. Then I started working back at the car wash. I had to move in with my parents again at 21 years old. I worked at the car wash for about two years, making $9/hour. The most I ever made was $10.50/hour, with an occasional $250/month bonus. I was working 60 to 75 hours per week. And I have the paycheck stubs to this day. One day, a lady came in and offered me a job in the mortgage industry. She said, "Every week I come in here. I try to buy a $10 wash. You sell me an $18 wash. Come work for me. You're in the wrong business."

I've always lived in a glass house. We're going to talk about the glass house of social media here, later on in the book, but I've always lived in a glass house. I told her, straight up, "Lady, I'm a felon. I don't own a credit card. That truck is paid for in cash and I rent an apartment. I don't know why in the world you would want me to work for you, giving financial advice to people, but I appreciate your generosity and the offer."

She said, "No, seriously. If you'll quit this job, at the car wash, I'll teach you how to be a millionaire by the time you're thirty." That's a pretty fucking strong proposition for a convict. That's a strong proposition for anybody at 22 years old.

Then one day, I got into a fight with the owner of the car wash. Not a fistfight, but a verbal disagreement. Afterward, I called that lady up and said, "Hey, I just quit my job. When can I come work for you?" She replied, "You can drive over here right now, if you want."
I did, too. I went straight to her office in my car wash clothes. Everybody in the

office laughed at me, and I didn't even know it. I was too stupid to know it. Well, I wasn't stupid. I was ignorant. I didn't know there was this whole other world. I'd come from a world where convicts dressed tough. You had muscles. You worked hard. You fought. You looked at people fucking sideways, and if they looked at you sideways, you'd punch a motherfucker in the face. When you're running the car wash, you got motherfucking degenerates coming off the street from halfway houses, parole houses and all these other fucking places. You can't be a pussy when you're running a car wash. It's 150 fucking degrees in Texas in July and you're washing 1,000 cars on a Saturday with motherfuckers used to starving to death. They'd steal quarters, diamonds, drugs and everything you could possibly imagine. I had to deal with it all, inside and out.

All of a sudden, I'd walked into an office where the politics were unfamiliar and everyone was relating in a whole fucking different way than I'd ever seen before. I've got boots and Wranglers on. The first thing this lady did was call me that evening and say, "Here's a couple hundred bucks. I want you to come pick up this card and go shopping at Express with Claude." Claude was the first openly gay person I ever met. He took me shopping and put me in some clothes that I, otherwise, would not have bought. When I showed back up at the office the next day, everybody realized how damn good looking I was, thanks to Claude. Claude also taught me the mortgage business. He showed me how to do some things to make ends meet and how to make sense of it all. He trained me and another guy, and remains my friend to this day.

I built up my sales. Within about six months of working for this place, I was the branch manager and top producer. I was kicking everybody's ass in the whole entire company by a landslide. I wasn't breaking rules like a lot of people were.

They would cut corners, do things backwards and forge documents. A lot of people in this company got in trouble for it, but not me, because I never did that shit. I operated the right way, because I had been to the fucking penitentiary. I swore to God, no matter how much money I ever made, I wouldn't do shit wrong again and go back to prison, because that was a fucked-up place. And I meant it.

I watched everybody else at first, make $50K, $60K, $100K each month. There I was, happy as a motherfucker, making $10,000. One day, I figured out the fucking key to all of it: a legit way to sell properties from builders to investors, at a profit, so everybody would be fucking happy. I did a shit-ton of those deals. I did so many, I stopped working for that particular company and bought a branch instead. I moved into an office right down the street from my new $400,000 home.

I worked out of my house for the most part, as I do now. This was long before social media, or at least before I knew of it, anyhow. At the first of the month, real estate agents would come over to pick up checks and sign documents. Title companies would come over to sign papers with me and tenants would do the same. At one point, I either managed, owned, or was involved in a partnership with more than 30 houses. I collected checks on all of them. At the time, I was doing 15 to 30 investment transactions a month and I was no longer a loan officer. Now, I was strictly pushing papers and making connections.

During this time, I had gotten married twice. The first marriage ended when she hit herself in the head with a pan then called the police on me. I won that case in court. It was really interesting. My second wife had been the first girl that I'd liked after the first falling out. I have this habit of going all-in to relationships. But I have always had this habit in every aspect of my life. It goes like this: "I like you. You like me. Let's go all-in together." It's just the way I am with business partners, girlfriends, wives and friends. So, while all these people are coming over, I've got an angry ex-wife running around. At the same time, I've got a new wife trying to figure all this stuff out, to see what's really going on. She's not sure what I do for a living. She's not sure how all this stuff works. She just knows we have good money and a lot of people coming around.

One day in 2004, my wife got pulled over by the police and had a joint in her car. I was unaware of them pulling her over and letting her go. Apparently, the police then started watching my house because of my prison history. Later that month, a tenant left my house and he was pulled over with drugs in his car. So, now that's two people; one that lives with me and a tenant, both leaving with drugs. It was a sure sign to the police to secure a warrant, because to them, there'd obviously been some drug dealing going on in my home.

One day, as I left the house, I saw a cop on a motorcycle. I waved to him and then he pulled us over and arrested me for a warrant from 1997. Remember, you guys, I've already done prison time in 1999. How could a warrant from 1997 interfere? I should walk out, off parole as a free man. When I got to the station, I found out I didn't have a warrant from '97, but that there'd been a hold on me from the FBI. I go up to this long room, cocky as fuck, knowing I ain't done nothing wrong. I've been minding the rules. They say, "Mr. Stewman, we've got your ass again. Internet identity theft, blah, blah, blah."

I'll be honest. At this time, I didn't know what the fuck the Internet really was and it confused me. I used email, and I might look at porn occasionally or download music, but that's about it. I'm like, "You got the wrong guy. I've never committed identity theft before. I don't even have a credit card." They pulled up pictures of a car from the local 7-Eleven camera surveillance tape. It was one of my tenants. The home he lived in happened to be the first home I'd ever lived in, in McKinney. While he'd been my roommate, for like a week, he'd introduced me to somebody else, before making an announcement about this new person: "Hey, Richard will take over your rent when you move out."

When I moved out and bought the nice $400,000 home, Richard moved into that home, and I guess, just left the Internet on. No big deal. I didn't know the dude was going to get all tweaked out on methamphetamine and tear off on this credit card theft bender. Anyway, I find all that out, and then the FBI realizes it's not me in the pictures. I tell them, "Hey, that's the house he rents from me. This is what I do for a living." I went through the whole thing and I figured my hands are fucking washed of all of it.

Also at that time, I have these really mad neighbors, because we like to party over at Casa de Stewman. The music gets loud and shit, so the neighbors would call the cops. Their bedroom window was right next to my pool. They can suck a dick then and they can suck a dick now. Regardless, the fuckers called the cops on me. A. lot. I was an annoyance. The cops thought I had gotten away with something. They were wrong about the identity theft, and now they're having to come over and tell me to turn my stereo down when it's really not ridiculously loud. It's a snafu. I know my rights, because I've done fucking time in prison and dealt with plenty of lawyers and shit…more than you could ever imagine.

One week, I went on vacation with my family, on a cruise from Galveston Island, Texas to Cancun, Cozumel, Playa del Carmen and back. I took my birth father, my grandparents, his parents, my aunts, uncles, cousins. I also took my then-girlfriend. Maybe she was my wife at this point, I don't remember, but regardless, she was number two.

When I took this vacation, we went to another country and came back to Dallas to stay on a Sunday night. Monday morning, I had to cash a check because I was out of money from blowing it all in Mexico. So, I cashed a check for $3,500. I owed $1,000 of it to my roommate, so I put the cash in the visor of my truck, lit up a blunt and fired off from Dallas to go home for the first time in a week.

When I arrived at my house that Monday afternoon, it looked like an ambulance was parked in front of my house with a bunch of other vehicles. It kind of freaked me out. As I got closer, I realized it didn't say "ambulance" on the vehicle. It said "SWAT." I pulled off to the right, where another police officer came with an M-16, telling me to get the fuck out of my truck. Then he proceeded to bust me in the head. The Allen police department hit me in the back, put me on the ground and handcuffed me. They hit my wife, threw her on the ground and handcuffed her, too.

Then they took us both to the house where my roommate was sitting in handcuffs. This was the same roommate from when I got in trouble in 1999, oddly enough. Remember, when I go all-in with somebody, I go all-in, unfortunately. Again, he didn't have a job and was just living off me. The first time, he didn't go to jail. He'd gotten no charges, nothing. This time though, he was there by himself.

I never lock my front door and they had thrown a flash grenade in my house that burned my carpet. They had torn my house upside down under the suspicion I was running a meth lab, because someone had gotten pulled over with meth in their car when they were leaving my place. To this day don't know who it was, but I have some suspicions. The police searched my house. I knew I didn't have a meth lab inside. Once they told me what the warrant was for, I got very smart with them. They arrested me for marijuana, but not the joint I'd smoked on the way, still in the ashtray of my truck. They got me for the quarter-ounce in the kitchen drawer.

And they also arrested me for felony possession of a firearm because of the gun my stepdad had given me, which he claimed was a gift for doing their mortgage, which I didn't even do…by the way. He just gave me a gun for whatever reason. And he gave my roommate a gun. In Texas, as a felon, you can have a gun five years after the fact. During that time, however, there was a mandate with the ATF and they were trying to arrest a lot of people on guns and drug crimes. I fell victim to that. When they arrested me for felony possession of a firearm, I beat the state case, so they turned me over to the ATF. Once again, I was sentenced to 15 months in federal prison.

I had gone from making hundreds of thousands of dollars in gross income to sitting in prison, again, and I had minded the rules! I should have fucking given up. I should have quit. I should have bitched about my situation. I should have fucking slit my wrists. I should have shot myself with the fucking gun I had, but I didn't. Two months in, wife number two cleaned me out. She sent me a letter telling me she'd hooked up with a boyfriend. While it wasn't the first one she'd had since I had been gone, it was the first one she'd been in love with and they were going to get married, spend my money and use my furniture, blah, blah, blah. She even sold all my houses. I had given her power of attorney. She was my wife, after all. That was the whole point behind it. But she left me with nothing. Fifteen months later, I got out of prison with $600 to my name that my birth father had left on my books. At 28 years old, I had to move in again with my adopted dad and mom.

That's when things changed for me. I remember when I got off the train one day from coming in from the halfway house, and my adopted dad saying, "This is the last time we're going to do this song and dance." That's what I remember thinking at the time: "Motherfucker, it was your motherfucking gun that got me into this fucking situation." But I knew I needed a place to stay, so I just apologized. It was the story of my life. They would do shit and I would suffer the consequences of it.

I was all-in.

I did a couple of odd jobs, thinking I'd never be able to do loans again. Then I got a job, through a friend, at the biggest bank/mortgage lender privately owned in the state of Texas. Despite my criminal record and every reason they tried to give me not to hire me, I overcame their objections, and promised, demanded, over-delivered and even worked on Saturdays. Within two months, I ran that motherfucker, too. They would talk behind my back. "He's got a felony. He looks like he's on steroids. He smokes pot. He fucking takes pills. He drinks." But always in the end: "He can fucking close."

They couldn't hold a candle to me, so no matter what the fuck I did, I ran that shit. I don't say that to be egotistical. I just say it to show you it doesn't matter where you come from. Your past or how you're brought up doesn't matter. You can go all the way to the top, and then go to the fucking top of the top, if you put yourself into it. It's not like this shit just happened to me. I worked eight hours a week, where these other motherfuckers worked twenty. I worked Saturdays, where these other motherfuckers didn't even work on Fridays. I asked for more leads when everybody else was telling me the leads they had sucked. I called everybody ten times when everybody else didn't even email them.

I put systems in place, and every time I succeeded, made note of it. Every time I learned something new, I made notes, because the rules had changed when I was in federal prison. The economic and mortgage meltdown had happened. I went in making easy money, in 2007, and came out at the end of 2008, where 100 percent financing and stated income didn't exist anymore. For those of you who know, it was a whole different game. So, I had to learn a new way of writing "government loans" and excelled to the top in that specialty, writing loans legally, because I was sponsored. I worked my ass off to be at the top. And I put a team in place, too.

About two weeks before starting that job, I got a message on Facebook or Myspace. I had just signed up for it. It was from a girlfriend I'd had when I was nineteen. Yep. *That* girl. She said, "Hey, I see you're divorced again. Great job there, pal." A couple seconds later, she said, "Oh, got to go. My dog just got sprayed with a skunk." I ended up closing her to meet me from Myspace or Facebook, whichever it was. I knew that my ex-wife was watching me on social media, so I started bragging about the trophies I had gotten and about the amount of people I had helped. I was boasting about the money I made and my beautiful girl. I would even brag about the new cars I was buying, because I wanted her to remember whoever she was with would never be like me, at least in that sense. Because of that, people saw me as the expert. They said, "Damn, Ryan knows a lot about this mortgage shit. Let me get on some loans." I started receiving messages all day. Emails and chat messages from Facebook, saying, "Ryan, can you do my loan?"

I knew I was onto an idea. I even started selling other stuff through social media, to make side income, because I knew something huge was about to break with Facebook. This was in 2009. In 2010, the Dodd-Frank Act was passed. It changed the game for me. I wasn't allowed to write loans anymore because I was a felon. I could no longer be in that business anymore without having to cut corners. I had plenty of brokers offering me side deals, under-the-table deals, let-me-originate-it-in-my-name deals. But I told you, I've always tried to mind the fucking rules, aside from the pot-smoking thing, ever since I did my first stint. I learned my lesson early.

I started selling this, that and the other. I wanted to manage social media. I knew something was going to pop. I bought Kate Buck Jr.'s *Let's Get Social* program, because I knew she had already done what I saw myself doing. I followed her guidance on that program. While I didn't take the same paths she did, I knew I could use what I'd learned from that program to help people in the mortgage and real estate industry, which is exactly what I did. It's what's gotten me to where I am today.

When you're out there, and you say, "I can't kick ass because of this. I can't kick ass because I drink. I can't kick ass because I don't have my shit together at home. I can't kick ass because I'm broke. I can't kick ass because I don't have money. I can't kick ass because I'm divorced. I can't kick ass because I'm a felon. I can't kick ass because I'm fat. I can't kick ass because I'm out of shape. I can't kick ass because I'm black. I can't kick ass because I'm white. I can't kick ass because I don't have any legs." Man, Fuck that. If I can do this shit, you can do it, too. It's all about having a mentality. I should have failed. I was given almost every reason there is on this planet to fail. Everything people tell you, "You're going to grow up and be a loser, be bankrupt, divorced and in prison..." I should have quit. But what happens when you quit? You're still playing the fucking game. You're just the last one picked. What happens if you quit? You're still stuck in life; you just suck at life more. Let me share with you what's allowed me to kick ass because I think kicking ass is important.

It's not so much that I have a competitive mentality, it's that I want to prove to myself I'm not what people told me I always was, what my parents told me I was, what giving me up for adoption told my psychological self. I want to prove to myself I can do what needs to be done. I can succeed. I figure the best way to do that is to service people above and beyond their wildest expectations.

When I sold all those car washes, people would come in and they would want a $10 car wash. I would explain to them that for four more dollars, just 50 percent more, we can do 200 percent more to their car, where they wouldn't have to wash it as fucking often, and it would actually save them money. I'm not very good at math and I don't know if what I'd said was true or not, but it really fucking worked at the car wash. I showed them I could provide a better service for them, and I could go above and beyond their expectations, if they were willing to pay for it. And they were.

The same thing applied in the mortgage business. It's not that I have the cheapest rates, the cheapest fees, the cheapest programs or even the best programs. It was the fact that if people wanted to talk to me, I answered my cell phone at midnight. If they wanted to make sure their shit went through smooth the first time, they knew I was the guy good with paperwork. Never once did someone that bought a million-dollar house from me, ask me how much money I made a year. Never once did someone ask me what my credit score was, and let me tell you, it was fucked because I'd been in and out of prison. All they cared about was me solving their problem, and the service level I could provide to them. I've been available selling drugs via beepers. I've been available selling mortgages via text message. I've been available selling consulting on social media. The bottom line is that I want to make sure I'm there to service the crowd, wherever the crowd may be.

If you're going to kick ass, you've got to have the mentality of going above and beyond everybody else. If you're going to kick ass, you've got to be a bad motherfucker. If you're going to be a bad motherfucker, you should be able to stand among your competition and call them out. You've got to have a mentality that it's in your best interests to help your clients succeed even more than you succeed. When I see my clients making more money than me, I get really fucking excited. A) it's a chance for me to level up and B) it's a chance for me to see the magnificence they are applying to their lives.

I have the mentality to where, when someone comes into my sphere and they buy a product, I give them bonuses. If you get this book, you see the extra shit I've given you throughout this book. This is a book and yet you're able to put million-dollar ideas together and hear a story of inspiration, all from a cheap-ass book. This is how I've always excelled to the top, through service and giving.

The giving part is huge.

When I first got started in the social media, Internet marketing space, I knew I had to make a name for myself and get exposure. The only way to do that was to start putting stuff out there on the Internet. If you're going to put something out there, it's got to be worth watching, or it'll just sit out there. You'll have wasted your time, digital space and everything in between. Right? I started making videos of how I closed sales. I would record my sales calls, talk about all my sales tricks, write free e-books and do everything I could on a daily basis. My third ex-wife would get so frustrated with me because I would spend literally 15 hours a day creating content, writing blog posts and making videos. That was on top of the time I spent at other jobs I was working to hold the whole thing together. I worked at car dealerships and at title companies. I did odd jobs, anything I could do, just to crush deals. I helped the handicapped get jobs at huge Fortune 500 companies. Everything I could to be able to make money to provide for my family. While I was working on creating all this content and letting people know that I was going to be here to stay, I went over and above. I was so dedicated to giving to everybody. I'd give it away on Facebook and on every social media site out there. I remember when I was first getting started, I was looking for traffic any which way I could get it. Every time I saw that somebody clicked, viewed, or looked, I became so excited I couldn't sleep that night. I just wanted to create more and get more out of it.

I couldn't get views telling people, "Call me if you want the secret." I had to give it all away right then and engage people. The lesson I've learned is you can give away just about anything. You know how to write a book, but the reason you haven't written one is that you don't have anybody holding you accountable and you just haven't taken the time to do it. I started giving everybody everything, to where they would reach out to me and say, "I saw your video on this. What are you doing now? Let's talk about that. What are you trying to use it for?" I would walk them through a powerful sales conversation, to ultimately lead them into becoming a paying client. I would do that over, and over, and over again. I took on business partners. At one point, I was managing 70 social media accounts. I was writing five posts a day for each of my clients. It was like hundreds of thousands of posts we did at one time, for everybody. A massive amount of social media.

Then one day, I pulled the plug on it all. I said, "No more doing. I've proven that I can do it. I've done it all my life. I worked all the way to be the number one mortgage guy. I worked all the way to become that guy in the mortgage industry niche on social media. It's time that I pull out and start teaching people what I did, how I think and what I do. It's time I show them how to apply it to their business."

I started off with real estate agents and loan officers. Just giving massive content away at hardcorecloser.com. I gifted videos, writing and email scripts. I was putting it all out there on that website, because I knew the way to break into my current business was to continue creating content every spare second. Just keep creating content, like I'm doing right now, as I write this book.

You might say, "How do you that, Ryan? If I'm going to give all that stuff away, how do I find out what to give to my niche" Well, what are they looking for? What do you wish you could find when you Google things about the niche you're in? Remember the questions you had when you first got started in your industry? Answer those on video. Put them on YouTube and watch motherfuckers come, because there are other people with those same questions, too.

You say, "Well, Ryan, I don't have time to create all that content. I've got a job." So did I. I worked at a car dealership. When I was sitting in the front waiting for UPS to come in, I would type in my Evernote account. For my next blog post, I would make videos in the car parking lot. My boss respected it, too. You know why? Because I sold more fucking cars than anybody else.

Here's what you need. You need routines in your life. I have routines in mine. I wake up at 5:00 AM, so I can be at 6:00 AM CrossFit or the gym, then I'm back home by 7:30 AM. I have a breakfast routine, hang out with the family for five or 10 minutes and then immediately head into my office to start creating content. At

10:00 AM every day, I have a meeting. That means I've got to stop creating content, and go into my phone meetings, or Google hangouts, or whatever I'm doing. From there, I have meetings all the way up until 2:00 PM, where once again, I break free to start creating content for two more hours. Then I'm done for the day; and this happens every single day of the week. Except for Sunday.

If I need to add something new to my routine, like read a book daily, I add it to my calendar. I've gotten to where I just add everything on my Google calendar because then it stays on my iPhone. I can look on my calendar the night before, and see what I've got for the next day. As soon as I wake up in the morning, alarm-free because I don't need one, I check out the calendar and see what I've got for the day ahead.

It's all about routines. You know what? Sometimes you wake up after a holiday. Sometimes you wake up after a long night of partying, or a fun day of partying and you don't want to get after work. That's when you need to push the hardest. That's when routines pay off the most. When it hurts is when you're supposed to fight the most. If someone hits you and it hurts, you better fight back twice as hard. It's the same way with life. When life gives you a headache, you better get to sweating, and shake that bitch off because it's your job.

If you're going to kick ass on all fronts, you're going to have to kick ass at work, kick ass at home, kick ass in your fitness and kick ass in your spirituality. You're going to have to crush it in video, social media, text messages, emails and autoresponders.

These days, if there's something out there you're not taking advantage of—I'm not talking shiny object syndrome—I mean, if there's something out there you're not taking advantage of, you're missing out. If you're not using video on Facebook and

YouTube, you're missing out because someone else is doing it. If you're not tweeting, you're missing out because someone else is using Twitter. If you're not close to LinkedIn, you're missing out, because someone else is sharing relevant shit. If you're not posting to Google+, you're missing out, because someone else is. If you're not on Facebook, making sure you chat with people, you're missing out because someone else is doing what you are supposed to be doing.

Sounds exhausting doesn't it? It is, but once you put it in place, you find yourself in a routine where it becomes just like an exercise regimen. It was hard the first time, but if you do it in chunks: day two, day three, day four, day five, you get better and better at it. It's just like, "Oh well, I've got to do this. No big deal." Then, all of a sudden, you can add to it. You can complicate things, compound them, or whatever. If you're going to kick ass, you've got to crush on all fronts.

In the next chapter, I'm going to teach you the strategy to kick ass, take names, emails and phone numbers. How to collect them, what services I use, what follow up programs are best, what to say to prospects and so forth.

See you in the next chapter.

PART TWO

HOW TO TAKE NAMES, EMAILS AND PHONE NUMBERS

Before I tell you my story of how I came from the very bottom, without anything and started over for the second time, let me tell you a little bit about why I was forced to do this. Let me tell you why the ships were burned, so to speak. (That's an old phrase. When you are going to attack somebody on an island, you burn the ships behind you).

In 2005, the local police kicked through my front door because they suspected I was manufacturing methamphetamines. I did not manufacture, sell, or use methamphetamines at that time. That's not saying I have never done that, but at that time in my life, I was surely not partaking. They kicked in the door because they were honestly wondering why I had realtors, investors, renters, loan officers and everybody else coming over to my house. I worked out of my home, just like I do now. The police got curious and obtained a warrant because of my past drug history. They broke into my home. Obviously, they didn't find drugs, but they did find a gun.

So, they offered me a sentence of 25 years, which I fought off for two years. The guy representing me as my lawyer just so happened to get elected as the first black Dallas County District Attorney. I believe he used me as a bargaining chip. I don't know how it all worked. I could be wrong in my hunches, but I know the fact he won had a big influence on the amount of time they gave me. I was handed a 15-month sentence.

From March or April, 2007, I sat in federal prison in Seagoville, Texas. And while I was stuck there, I read a book I'd found somewhere or that somebody had sent to me called *Scratch Beginnings*. There's really no sense of significance in the book. It was a story about a kid who left the town he lived in, left his parents and everything, with just the clothes on his back, and 200 bucks. He had no toothbrush, no toothpaste, only 200 bucks. He had to spend some of that 200 on a plane or train to get to whatever city he wound up in. He went to the counter and found the cheapest ticket to Charleston, South Carolina, which was like two states over. He started over again with nothing.

He got a job with a moving company, and worked his way up by busting his ass. Eventually he became the manager, then he started his own moving company, which became a very successful business. His whole new history began when he left home with just 200 dollars. At one point, he actually earned enough money to move his family near him and he even hired some of them. It was inspiring to me. I thought if this guy could do it, then maybe it wasn't a fluke that I had made a little bit of money before. Maybe, just maybe, I could do it, too.

One night I had a dream. I'm not a person who remembers dreams, or is an interpreter of dreams, or any of that fancy stuff. I don't even remember most of my dreams. But I remember this one. The dream was so vivid I woke up, and shook my cellmate, urging, "Wake up, man. I've got to tell you about this dream." Well, you know, people in prison are not the most cheerful early risers at two in the morning. It's not like he was my spouse or some shit, right? Anyway, he's like, "Man. What do you want, dude? What do you WANT?" I said, "Listen. I had this dream." Then I began to tell him about it. I was sitting in a bar, but I wasn't drinking alcohol. I was drinking water. It was the weirdest thing. I look over at two girls, and they're giggling and having drinks; they're talking. I say, "Is there a particular reason you two are laughing at me?" And they reply, "You're Mr. Right Now." I asked them, "Oh, so you read my books?"

Then I woke up. That was it.

I was like, "Man, I think I'm going to write a book one day." Back then that was always my saying: "Do it right now! Let's go right now! Call them right now!" It was what I would always say to rev myself up. I even have a motivational video entitled *Right Now*. But the *Scratch Beginnings* book and the dream showed me I had something bigger to do.

I didn't really think much about the dream after that, until one day in 2011. I was sitting at a bar, drinking water, and two girls down the bar said, "Hey, you're the Hardcore Closer. You're the guy who does that Internet stuff." *How cool was that*?

It all started with marketing. I knew there was a good chance, when I was sitting in federal prison that I was not going to be able to get a mortgage license. I knew I was going to have to rely on some sort of marketing. I knew it wasn't going to be an opportunity that had fallen in my lap, but one I would have to claw my way toward. When I was released from prison, I had to live 12 days in a halfway house. It wasn't enough time to get a job so I was stuck there, with mind-boggling boredom. I had to think about what I was going to do for those 12 days. I had to put some kind of plan together. I remembered when I was a teenager in the dope game, the other guys would always say, "Man! How are you moving so much? How are you selling so much weed? How are you selling so much coke?" I usually said something like, "Well, you know, man I don't rely on people to just hit me up. I have a list of people that generally buy from me and I send them a message, or I beep them with my code about once a week to make sure they hit me up and don't go somewhere else. "I was branding myself. Of course, I probably said some fly shit more like, "Yo, dog! You know what? I'd just be running shit." Because that's how I talked then. That's how I talk now. But before I realized it, I was marketing. I would call people up Saturday afternoon to ask, "Hey man, do you need anything before you go out tonight?" or "Hey man, do you want to do this?" or "Drop by before you go out man, I'll give you a free (something) with that."

I was always trying to give to people. One time, I inherited a bunch of acid for free when I bought some weed to sell. So, I shit you not, I ran a special, instead of trying to get greedy with money, I advertised: "Come over, buy an ounce and get a hit of acid for free." Always marketing. When I got in the mortgage game in 2003, nothing had really changed. I was still marketing.

I ended up doing the first loan for a friend of mine, who had known me through the drug and prison days. Just sitting there watching a Sunday afternoon game at their house, we did the deal. The second loan was from the landscape guy, who had bought a $700,000 house. He owned the landscape company responsible for mowing the yard of a car wash.

It all happened because I reached out to people. I talked to people. And I always,

always, always have an angle. Fast-forward to 2008. I'm at the end of my prison sentence, and I'm out on the street with nothing. I had twelve-hundred dollars to my name. I had to move in with my stepfather and my mother, begrudgingly, in a home I had helped them secure financing for. Now I was sleeping in the guest bedroom. It was especially humbling the first day I was picked up from the halfway house off the DART rail station I'd ridden into North Texas. My stepfather looked over at me and said, "Hey, we're going to make sure this doesn't happen again because if it does, I won't be there to pick you up." So, I had just burned another bridge. There was no hope for me. I didn't want to live with my parents, but next time I wouldn't even have them if I didn't start to make some right decisions. To do something right. The first thing I did was start making phone calls to let people know I was out and available for work. Then I got a couple of offers, and I learned a lesson.

Thank God, I learned this lesson in the early phase of the game, because it would have been much more exhausting. The lesson was to decipher bullshit offers from real ones. In the beginning, I didn't know the difference. I did this deal for this company, we'll just call them T.U.C. So, T.U.C. would have me head out to people who own their home. We would go in the home, and they would deed their property over to T.U.C., who would then pay the property off. The homeowners would get the property for free, but they were also expected to make some kind of effort in the community or whatever.

Turned out it was some kind of anti-government Ponzi scheme. I don't even know how in the world I dodged that bullet. I could have gotten in a lot of trouble at some point if I would have really blown up from that. But it wasn't all it was cracked up to be, honestly. Ain't nothing fun about giving everybody's checks back that came to me. It was just a pain in the ass. Could've possibly killed my credibility, too. But I learned a lesson: not every opportunity is an opportunity. Sometimes what seems too good to be true, is exactly that.

I pressed on. Took a recruiting job for an insurance agency. I'd never even had any insurance on anything other than a house and a car. I knew nothing about it and I wasn't ready to take the test because I wasn't sure what exactly they wanted me to do. I couldn't get any training either, so I failed again.

I still had only $1,200 in my account and my Dodge truck had been sitting still for a year. All four tires went out on it. As you know, tires are expensive and they were 22-inch rims back bought in the days I'd had money. But I was broke now, and I had to trade my truck in with four flat tires. I took a huge loss on it in order to finance a car, so I could skip a month of payments, not ruin my credit and even get a full tank of gas without having to spend a dime. The deals I worked to survive weren't just to sit back and let somebody come take my truck. I thought of a clever way to keep everybody happy. The dealership won. They fucked me over on money, but at the time I was happy because I got what I wanted. The lenders were happy as well, because everything was paid on time.

I did everything I could, until one day, I heard from a guy I knew from the old school mortgage business I had worked for before I went to prison. While I was in federal prison, my wife left me, cleaned me out and then she took over my job and told coworkers a bunch of terrible stories about me. So, after prison, I didn't have anywhere to go. Fast-forward over to where we are now. The same guy that used to work at the old company has a new place and he says, "You should really come check this out. They're the largest privately owned bank in the state of Texas doing mortgages."

I went in and interviewed for the job, with the general manager. It went down like this, "We can talk all day about my qualifications as a mortgage officer, but the truth is I've been in the federal penitentiary the last 15 months. You're not going to find it on my record. But if you run background, you'll find I did state time when I was nineteen. My last tax returns look like this." I had brought the returns with me. My last paycheck stub in the mortgage business before I went to prison looked like this: and I gave him the stub. In the midst of my honesty, I also said, "I know this is a self-generated business. If you will give me a chance, I will more than double and quadruple those numbers and never disappoint you. If you take a chance on me, you won't regret it."

We had an hour and a half conversation about how fucking cool it was going to be for me to work there, and I started the next week. I sold everything, convinced if they would give me just one chance, I would make them believers. In three months I was the top producer of that mother fucker, making believers of them all. I built a team of two assistants and a processor and generated hundreds of thousands of dollars of revenue for the company, millions of dollars in closed mortgage commissions and millions of dollars in junk fees. That lasted only18 months, because in 2010, the world came to a crash again for me when the passing of the Dodd-Frank Act no longer allowed convicted felons to originate mortgages. It was as if I had been released from prison all over again. By this time, I had married ex-wife three and moved into her house. We had bills to pay, cars and a mortgage. All were my responsibility because she wasn't working anymore. Shortly after we got married, she had quit her job, and now I was losing mine.

People were offering me opportunities everywhere, but I was scared to take them. I didn't want to go back to prison. I didn't want to get caught cheating, because we knew they would point the finger at me. I had to do something. Some people I knew from church, who I considered friends and who also appeared successful in multi-level marketing (MLM), (but really weren't) seemed like a good bet. Then I learned again, every opportunity isn't what it seems to be. I'm not here to knock MLM or anything else. You do what you want to with it. I'm just telling you the experience I had where people weren't making the amount of money they claimed. People weren't doing the amount of work they said they were doing. When it got to where I had worked up and was making the amount of money I wanted to make, they pulled the rug out from under me and jerked my commission, Understandably, I got mad at the industry.

Just like the loan officer industry, and after such a rude surprise, I didn't know what to do. But I *did* have a contact database via Facebook that I had been building since I had gotten released from prison in 2008. The database contained the names of everybody I had ever done loans for. So, I did have a way to reach out to people, because I had always collected information. We're in two businesses as sales people. We're in the information-collecting business, and the lead-generation business. That's all. Nothing more, and nothing less. There's a big difference between a lead and information.

Information is a name, address, email and phone number. A lead is a name, address, phone number and email of somebody who has a high probability of purchasing your stuff.

The first thing I did was buy an information product and that's when I learned about the online community of rebels called Internet marketers. People who were making money left and right just by using the Internet.

As I dove more into the game, I found out it took a lot of hard work, a lot of knowledge and a lot of time. This wasn't just sales; I was learning a whole new trade from the beginning. I had to do it. I went night and day, night and day, night and day, consuming all the information I could, soaking up WordPress, social media, Twitter and LinkedIn. I bought programs and invested in educational tools until I had blown my entire savings and my wife's, too. Then I borrowed money from my in-laws in order to immerse myself with this information. One day, I joined a program for $8,000 I really didn't have. But it changed the game for me. It put things in perspective. It allowed me to commune with a mastermind of smart people. A place I could learn from multiple people in one place at one time. I heard what was working for them and what wasn't. I learned what drove them and how they acted. These were successful people, all in one place. It was like a fucking test case experiment for me, and it was the best investment I had ever made.

When I had started in real estate in 2005, I wound up exiting because of the whole police business. When I left the mortgage business for a while, I focused on buying and selling real estate for investors and things of that nature. A no-money down real estate course had started that ball rolling, too. In the future, I thought, when all else fails, I would build from that no-money down real estate course. I would make hundreds of thousands of dollars, maybe millions of dollars over the next decade.

I still succeed today from the lessons I learned from that course. So, I also figured out when all else failed, I would line up with a mentor who was doing exactly what I wanted; I would grab their fucking belt loop and follow them everywhere they went. And that's precisely what I did.

I did this with money I borrowed from my in-laws. It was all very humbling to say the least. I'd blown all of our money. I didn't have a job. My in-laws didn't know I was a two-time convicted felon. That's when I told them the whole story. They said, "It doesn't matter Ryan, we love you. We love you, no matter what." At that point, I felt so liberated.

I thought, "Well, if I can share this with them, it's time I come out and tell people this is the deal." But I wasn't quite ready yet. I didn't make an announcement on social media, because I was insecure since I hadn't been making any money. I was failing at everything I was doing. I had lost my life. It seemed like God was putting his thumb on me so hard to fail. The universe was pushing in every way it could against me. Sometimes I would say to myself in a deep prayer or deep meditation: "Motherfucker quit!" I would bang my head against the wall and stomp my feet. I started smoking weed every single day, all day. I don't know how I came up with the money. To this day, I haven't sold drugs again. But somehow I always managed to have a bag of weed. I would spend my last dime on it and just not eat, because I was losing my mind and I needed something to keep my cool. I didn't like to drink because I didn't like the hangovers, the headaches and what it does to your body. I don't like pills, so Xanax wasn't an option. I was smoking all day every day and losing my fucking mind. I was also $8,000 more in debt, with my in-laws.

So, I decided to join this program; this mastermind. They have a live event at the end of it, but I didn't have the money or the plane tickets to fly to the live event. God dammit anything these two guys that are running it tell me to do, I'm going to do it. So, we get into week one, week two, week three, then week four. I start making a few sales. I start making enough to cover the investment to get into the program. Then I start making a little profit. I kept everything on track. As I was building up the business, I met somebody once again with a golden opportunity, who got me side-tracked. These golden opportunities pop up all over your life. You'll think *this is great*! *This is the one I've been fucking waiting on. This is the shit I've been practicing for. It's game day, baby*! *This is the shit I've been doing my workout for every day.* Only to find out, it's all fucking bullshit.

I took a job with a title company. In that title company's office, they gave me pretty much no training and free will to do whatever I wanted, with no income. Stuck in the basement, I used their Internet every day, all day. I would stay late; I would lock the doors, and I don't think they even trusted me with the alarm code. I literally think they would have the office girl come back behind me. Regardless, they let me use their Internet and it was a quiet space for me to work, which I needed because I had moved in with my in-laws and rented my house out—I couldn't afford it anymore.

I started the Hardcorecloser.com domain in that office. I wasn't sure what the hell I was going to do with it, but I was going to make videos every single day. At the end of every one of those videos I was going to ask people to reach out to me, call me, text me, email me, or something. In every video, there would be a lesson to learn and a call to action. Today's lesson is on selling, tomorrow's lesson is on marketing, the third day it was on Facebook, the fourth day it was video. I stuck with it. Later that blog would become one of the top hundred-thousand blogs in the world, then it moved to the top fifty-thousand. At that time, I was starving to death and was so insecure, because I was living with my in-laws and renting my house out. It felt like I was living a lie under so much pressure. So many people depended on me and I felt like I couldn't admit failure because I would let them down.

I would tell my wife at night, "I'm losing sleep because I'm failing and there are people who think I'm winning. I can't afford to let them down because if I fail they'll use me as an excuse to fail." I slaved away at social consulting, working in a title company and putting on my program.

Teaching people social media in 2010 and in 2011 wasn't what it is today. I was turned down left and right. I would tell people, "Listen, you can make money from Facebook." They'd respond with a scoff, "Facebook! We don't allow our employees to play on Facebook!" I'd say, "You can make money from YouTube." They'd respond, "YouTube! We've got YouTube blocked."

In January 2011, we found out we were pregnant with my son, Jax aka Little-Man-Closer. We needed insurance, so I put everything else on hold again and took a job selling cars. Yes, it was a new opportunity and I wanted to sell cars, I just didn't want to work the hours that came along with it. I loved selling cars and learned so much from the experience. I'm going to tell you how it got me to where I am today. I sold cars for six months, just so I could have company insurance, in case something went wrong when Jax was born. I wasn't going to put our family's or Jax's life in any sort of tremendous jeopardy, so I got my friends to get me this job. And I passed my drug test somehow in less than forty-eight hours—because my body's really good at cleaning that stuff out, apparently.

I got on board, paid somebody to take all the tests for me, then I started selling cars. I sold them left and right, but I hated the cold calls. This company would collect information any which way. I was learning all sorts of different methods to make money, different ways to collect leads, different ways to be able to generate leads directly from the Internet and convert them. It was an amazing thing to watch, but it was a ton of hours. A. Ton. One day I got tired of cold calls. We were given a list of numbers to try and call. I got sick of bugging people and wasting time. You had to make thirty calls a day while working there. Some of you might be laughing at me, but I hated them, because cold calls aren't my thing. My thing has always been warm leads and networking. Still, I did it, and I was really good at it. I plowed through that inventory. Like everywhere else, before long I became a top producer, or second place, or usually in the top three. I earned bonus after bonus and sold a shit load of cars. I was very consistent. I worked my way up through the Internet department, then I thought: *you know what? I'm tired of this cold-calling. I just want to make videos and start sending emails with my videos*. In every one of my videos I would be in a different model of car. "Hey, I heard you were looking at a Ford Escape," or "Hey, I heard you were looking for a Ford Fusion."

I made videos for every single thing I could possibly think of because I had all this downtime. With the office and the car lot being right there, I used it wisely. I used it for innovation. When Jax was born I used it to get the hell out of there, too. I also used it as proof and said, "Hey, in this case we took in this amount of leads. We did this number of videos and got this amount of traffic." All of a sudden, I had data. Data meant I could go back to the same people, who turned me down for a social media consultancy, and say, "Look what I did, it's my personal business, and it's my sell. This isn't theory. This isn't bullshit. These are dollars I fucking made myself at a car dealership using Internet leads. You're a company that generates Internet leads." I knew I had their attention, so I kept going. "Let me show you how to turn your shit up using social media." I kept fighting. I was convicted. Eventually, somebody gave me a chance.

I took that client on contingency at a very low amount of money. I worked with them night and day. I did everything for them online and blew them up, which attracted a fellow out of nowhere. He told me that he had done hundreds and millions of dollars in real estate, and I didn't verify it. I had an opportunity arise, so I just jumped on. It got me sidetracked.

Over the next seven months, I would fight for people to let me run their social media for $100/month. I worked my way up to about seventy people. The company took a huge loss. I lost investors' money. The CEO was a fruitcake, whack-job, annoying, combative and contrary, everything you wouldn't want. It was total fricking chaos, with me and my wife doing all of the work, while paying somebody else. A bad sour partnership deal. False accounts, stolen money and money funneled overseas. I'm lucky I was able to save my reputation and I was smart enough to keep documented proof over the years so I could show people that I wasn't the one who had pulled the shenanigans.

I had to keep fighting the good fight. One day, when I'd had enough, I hired another mentor. That mentor allowed me into another mastermind. Through that mastermind, I learned more and I changed my business model again, into the one I'm about to share with you.

You are two businesses: the information-collection business and the lead-generation business.

It's your job, daily and hourly, to collect information that could ultimately turn into leads. Without people to talk to, you're not going to have any money, or any people to close. You need to understand the more hands you shake; the more money you make. You need to talk to people on Facebook. My personal marketing method for organic Facebook marketing goes like this: each week we use our lucky seven methods.

That means we post twenty-one different prospects a week. The lucky seven breaks down to: each week, you post on one person's wall, you send one person a private message and you leave a comment on at least one person's post that you see in the newsfeed, or in a behind-the-scenes group. By doing this, we are raising ad rates. We are getting seen in their newsfeed. We're bringing ourselves to them. We're being social. We're shaking hands. We're reminding them. Now I'm not talking about your best friend that you go to the club with on Friday night. I'm talking about somebody, anybody you are connected to and haven't talked to in a while on Facebook. You're going in and engaging them.

What typically happens, and what I've trained my personal clients to do, is to go into private groups or forum groups on Facebook and use those posts for commenting. Your job is to consistently generate leads and you need to have follow-up systems behind it. My personal recommendation is to make seven wall posts, seven comments on people's posts and seven private messages. We're not just talking random shit here, ladies and gentlemen. We're talking about seven people who you could potentially get a business referral from, or who can directly become a client of yours. It doesn't work by sending them a private message saying, "Hey, buy my shit." You see there's this little thing about Facebook called people's walls and being connected to people who have walls. Right? Yeah, walls and balls, baby. Being connected to people who have walls means being able to write on that wall. Being able to go to that wall means seeing what they've written about.

The whole motive behind social media is if somebody puts something out there, they want you to like it. They want you to comment on it. They want to be the center of the attention. That's why we put stuff on social media in the first place. Social media is there for you to be social. If somebody says something, they want to be acknowledged for saying it because nobody wants to be the kid standing by themselves at the end of the hall with no likes. That's the equivalent of Facebook.

When you send somebody a private message, you get to be a detective. You get to check out their wall and see what they've talked about lately. Say yesterday, they talked about going to the park with their daughter. That private message you send out to them doesn't start off with, "Hey, I'm in x-y-z business. Buy my shit," or "Hey, you could really use some of my x-y-z," which is an insulting fucking sales pitch. Instead, you hit them up with, "Hey, I see you spent the weekend with your daughter, man. It's good to see a dad doing the things they're supposed to do like you. There's very few of us out there, believe it or not, and I didn't really find this shit out until I got into this world. You ever experience something like that?" Start a meaningful conversation you know they will connect with, no matter what it is. It doesn't have to be deep, but if you know them, talk to them like you know them. You don't have be all formal. You don't have to be all uptight. Those aren't the cool people. When you go out, you don't want to hang out and do business with the people that are formal and uptight. You want to hang out with the people that make things happen and that are cool and loose. That's what you're there to appear as. Lighten the fuck up, will you?

After the dialog has gone on long enough via private chat, this gives you the opportunity at the right time to say, "How's business going?" Because that's where it always ends up. You've got to take it there in due time though, just like you would if you were in a social conversation about playing a volleyball game or having a beer at the bar with your homeboy. Eventually, it's like, "Hey. How's business going? How's business treating you?" How you talk to your buddy at the bar, or your contact on Facebook should be identical. The good news is, if you're prospecting correctly, their business is profitable for your business. If they're doing badly, help them. If they're doing well, help them to do even better.

It's that simple. Once you get into the selling state of mind of how you can help them and not yourself, and how what you sell benefits them (not how what you sell gets you a paycheck or earns you a commission), the faster and the quicker you'll get wealthy. It takes an abundance mindset to be in sales. People that get into sales with a scarcity mindset can't sell shit. It takes only one trait to sell and that's confidence. We're not selling products, services, goods, or anything else. We're selling certainty and confidence. We're selling assuredness that we can do what the fuck we say we can do. That's all we're selling.

It doesn't matter if it's white gloves, or the chick eating fucking popsicles, or whatever product or service. (By the way, did you know Eskimos in Alaska addicted to methamphetamines are easy to sell ice to?—for all you drug heads, that's a good joke for you). What's going on here is you're taking action to connect with these people with the seven private messages and the set of seven wall posts. Again, it's not like, "Hey Jack, just looking at your wall and thought I'd tell you that you should totally come get a mortgage from me." No. You're going to do some detective work and you're going to say, "Hey Jack, it looks like you have a lovely family and you live a really cool life, man. We should get together some time or have a chat. Message me if you want to set something up."

Boom! Congratulate them. Tell them they're doing great. Try this one: "Hey, I saw you won the award for top producer last month. Congratulations. You know what? It's awesome to see somebody work as hard as you and get the reward time and time again. You deserve it. You're a cool motherfucker. You go, homeboy." Then, they'll send you a private message back. Guaranteed. After the applicable conversation occurs, you can ask, "What can I do to help your business?"

The third seven is making sure you comment on at least seven people's different posts throughout the week. When you comment, you don't just say, "Boom," or "Thanks," or "Awesome," or "Great posts," or "Cool, Jim." You're looking to add value. Comment on a post in the Facebook group for real estate if you're in real estate. Engaging content ends in a question. If someone asks a question in the group, or someone asks a question on Facebook, or asks for a referral, you say, "Here is the answer to what you're looking for," and explain in detail as if that person were six years old, then ask, "What do you think about that?" Ask an engaging question.

If someone posts, "Hey, I'm trying to sell a home and I'm not sure whether I should charge six percent or four percent, what do you think about it?" You may comment, "Well listen, people that typically charge four percent end up being not as focused when they sell the house, which they could have just sold for six percent and not cost people's money, or time on the market in the first place..." So on and so forth. End your comment with an engaging bit like, "If you'd like to know a little bit more," or "Does this sound good to anybody else on this thread?" or "What are your thoughts?" That way they have the chance to express their opinion, which people on social media love to do. You've brought them back into the conversation and engaged them. Each time somebody engages with you on Facebook, it raises your EdgeRank to where they will see you more in their news feed. It gives you the chance to brand yourself in front of them.

If you do something like the triple lucky seven method here, to where you're consistently prospecting 84 to 92 brand new people per month, we're talking seven wall chats a week, seven private messages a week and seven comments a week on different people. These are 21 fresh people you're reaching out to every single week. You can't help but run into business if you shake that many hands. You could stand in front of Wal-Mart and shake that many hands and run into business, regardless of who you are, or what part of the country or world you happen to be in.

Now, we also believe in posting on Facebook at least once a day, but three times are recommended: morning, noon, and night. First thing when you wake up in the morning, we have a really simple method. Whatever's on your mind, talk about it. You see something on the news that's engaging, fine. The more people that like, comment, and chime in, the higher your EdgeRank and the more you are seen in the newsfeed. The more you're seen in the newsfeed, the more people notice your brand and the more you get leads. People that like, comment, reply and interact with your posts, especially if they're business related, are leads. You don't need to ask them for their email address and everything else. You're already connected to them on Facebook. Send them a private message and say, "Hey, I saw that you chatted on my post today. I see that you're really into x-y-z. If you'd like, I could answer any questions right now. Probably I've got something for free I could give you. Let me do something really cool for you, and if you like it..." Then when the time is right, you ask them for their business.

This can be everybody that reaches out to you, likes, or comments on Facebook. It doesn't just have to be the people that click the links you put out there and who fill in your information. I recommend you post one to three times each day, morning, noon and night. I personally post sometimes up to eight times in a day on my personal page and nobody ever complains from the over-posting because

I deliver value. I'm not saying buy my shit, even though I do occasionally say, "Buy my shit." We use a tactic called the whip method to be able to do that. My whip method goes like this: you post two to three things that are totally nothing about your business. This can include information from your personal life, something funny, politics, or anything engaging. When people like and comment on your other posts, then you've earned the right to mention something for business. Business posts don't have to be, "Buy my shit." A business post on Facebook can read like: "It was so awesome to close this deal with the Smith's this weekend and watch their dreams come true. Everybody feel free to congratulate them and make them feel special for what we've done together."

I love my job. We're the information-collection business and the lead-generation business. What is information today may become the lead tomorrow. So how do you collect leads? My favorite method is the video-to-Wufoo form method. It's simple. I turn the camera around on my iPhone, point it on myself, hold it in front of me and make a simple selfie video. I make these videos using what I call the Jesus method. For all of you religious folks, don't freak out on me here. The Jesus method means 1) you learn a lesson, 2) you take an experience, 3) extract the lesson from it, and 4) share the experience and the lesson with people on video with a call to action. It's that simple. That's what Jesus did. He took everyday life experiences and turned them into parables. That's what I do, too.

For example, the video I posted on Facebook was about my CrossFit coach, who is 29-years old. He owns two highly successful businesses. He's up at 3:30 in the morning, six days a week for his CrossFit job. Then he goes off to a construction job during the day for a separate company he owns. In the evening, he comes back for three more hours to continue his CrossFit job. He's

24/7 but he's 29-years old and a very successful entrepreneur. So many people would just go to the gym to work out every day and never think that the guy who's training them is an entrepreneur. So many people never take a second to feel that experience, extract the lesson from it and share it with the general public. When you can do that, then people say things like, "Oh, I like that experience." "Wow, that's impressive." "Damn, I need to get my shit together." "Fuck," and a bunch of other expressions like: "Good for him. It's great to see that." "Faith renewed. I thought the younger generation was full of lazy slobs." And so on and so forth.

If you're good on camera, with more practice, you'll be even better. Eventually, you'll be able to make people laugh...or cry, if that's your thing. You can use video in powerful ways with this method I'm about to share with you, concerning how to capture information, but you must understand first the evolution of communication and the part videos play.

I was born in '79 and back in the 80's, cell phones arrived on the scene and people said, "Oh no, I don't want to give my cell phone number out for business purposes because I don't want people contacting me, other than my friends, family members and so on." People had this scarcity mentality, but at some point a smart salesman or two did some math and said, "Hey. For the amount of money I earn, I'm going to make sure I'm here to serve my people 24/7. I'm going to make sure I'm available for my people no matter what they want: 24/7. So, I'm going to give them my cell phone number. If they want to get in touch with me, they can get in touch with me. I have no problem with that."

And they did. Eventually everybody was forced to give out their cell phone number. Those who were early adapters cornered the marketing, and killed it for years before the others caught on to it. The same thing happened in the 90's. Emails arrived on the scene and people said, "I'm not going to give my email out. I don't want the Canadian Pharmacy, spam, porn, all this other stuff. I don't want to give my business email out, or I don't want to give my personal email out. It's just not safe." Then smart salespeople adapted and said, "You know what? I'm going to give my cell phone number and my email address out. I'm going to put it on the Internet so people in other countries can connect with me when they need access to me. I'm here to serve the people that deserve to work with me and I am here to win this game and be accessible 24/7."

Gradually, every company, every entrepreneur, everybody, had their name and email address on a website somewhere. If they didn't, they were fucked. The trend continued in 2000. When text messages came into existence, people said, "Well, send me a text message," and the response from the other person would literally be, "Oh, man. I don't want to text. Just call me." You have to understand, if the public is demanding to be communicated with in one way, you can't fight it. You've got to go with the flow. You've got to surf. You can't fight against the tide. You've got to get on your board and ride. You've got to be the one to hop on the wave and ride it and embrace it. Get comfortable on it. Get balanced on it. Get involved with it. When it ends, be the first one to catch the next wave. That's how it works. As a guy who's into surfing, I look at business that way, too. So, text messages rolled around, but people were still making phone calls.

In 2012, AT&T reported that 86 percent of all cell phone calls went unanswered, yet people were still saying stop texting me or trying to connect with me on Facebook. Meanwhile, text messages are 100 percent read. Facebook messages are 100 percent read. People are 86 percent not reachable with cell phone numbers and they're still trying to get in touch with them? The days of the cold call are dead. The days of communicating via telephone, unless you find yourself in absolutely paramount, dire, life-or-death circumstances, are dying. You've got to get good selling on a video. You've got to become a quick typist. You've got to be speedy when texting. You've got to be able to sell not just over the phone and not just face-to-face, but through your fingertips and words via text, email and private chat on Facebook. You've got to learn how to use Google Hangouts and FaceTime to get your video chat in front of prospects.

You've got to leverage technology. The time is coming that if you don't do it, you're going to be left behind. When I started this in 2009, and again in '10, '11 and '12...people would say, "Oh, my Facebook. Man, it's just for me and my family members." Meanwhile, people are making millions of dollars a month using Facebook organically.

I know them. Those who didn't embrace it in the beginning look like an ass now and are trying to swim to catch up with the wave so they can ride it. Meanwhile, those who were at the front of it, myself included, are enjoying the nice view from on top of the board. Now, ladies and gentlemen, I'm telling you, the next wave of communication, the next evolution, the next step in this matter is videos. If you're not making videos, you will be left behind. I don't care if you're fat. I don't care if you're ugly. I don't care if you're missing teeth or tattooed. I don't give a shit. You need to get that mug of yours in front of the video camera and give them the information they're dying for. Give them the Jesus experience. The Jesus method will help you. Go to a website called Wufoo.com and create an account. There you'll find a survey application that's easy to use, that you can drag and drop for free. Tell them I sent you. You can use it for people to enter in their name and information. So, you have a video and it works like this. This guy is 29-years old, owns a CrossFit, and gets up at 3:30 in the morning. It's no wonder he looks good. It's no wonder he makes money. It's no wonder he owns two successful businesses. Here's a guy with absolutely everything and if you want to be like Lee, and you want to have everything as well, then you just click the link next to his video, fill out this form and you and I will have a conversation. We'll have a phone conversation, Facebook, private chat, whatever you want to do to communicate because I want to communicate your way. I will help you. Just click the link. It doesn't matter what you're selling. Extract the method. Take the experience. Extract the lesson. Share it with them. Relate it to something, and give them a call to action. It's really simple.

You've got an easy strategy. Post one video a day to Facebook. By all means, post one video per day on YouTube, as well. People make the same comment to me over and over, "My YouTube account, it's just for me, man. It's just for my family." Open it up. People want to see you. We've been programmed all our lives. We've been sat in front of a television set and taught, "Hey, whoever's on that TV screen is important. Watch them." Well, now you have a chance to be more important with your cell phone. You'll be the one on that TV (cell phone) gaining the same authority and influence because so many people are scared to do it. This gives you a huge advantage! The number two fear behind falling is public speaking. If people are scared to speak publicly, that also means people are afraid to get in front of the video camera. You have a giant opportunity and a massive crowd dying for your content right at your fingertips on Facebook.

Just post a video, a few words and a link, so you can capture their information and find out if they're a lead or not. I've told you how. I've told you why and I've given you the method. In the next part, I'm going to talk to you about sales and about the conviction it's going to take.

If you're a person similar to me, you're someone who has faced adversity. I was a felon, a convict. I had to overcome a drug addiction. Whatever it is, maybe you've had to sell over a lot of objections, I'm going to teach you my mindset. The only mindset you need. I'll tell you why it works and the psychology behind it so you can be a Closer, too. See you in the next section.

PART THREE

THE CLOSER

So far, this book has been all about my story of survival, and the things I did. Now allow me to help you take the tools and experiences I have gone through, so you can learn from them and step up your game.

What can you tell about a mindset? The reason why you have or have not is because of the way you think. So, it would be really easy for me, with all the excuses I have, to sit around with a poor-me pity party. "I've been adopted. I've been arrested. I've been imprisoned. I've been divorced over, and over, and over. I can't seem to get shit together in my personal life. I continue to have family businesses that didn't work out."

Instead, I push on with as much integrity as absolutely possible and with as much discipline as absolutely necessary. We live in a very, very, very cold world, whether you want to have some skewed hipster view of it or not. Everything on this planet can and will kill you if you give it a chance. You could be walking down a flight of stairs at your house, apartment, or job and trip, fall, hit your head and die instantly at any given moment. Something could fall from the sky. You could get in a car accident. You have to reflect on what you would leave behind if your life ended instantly.

Would you be missed for a minute? Would you be missed for a month? Would you be missed for a millennium?

The mindset you have to adopt is you're ready to win and that you're not going to let the people around you and the world you live in dictate how to roll in this life. You're not going to let it tell you what you can't do. I've been told I couldn't do stuff my entire life. I've been told, "Ryan, you can't do that. You're a felon. Ryan, you can't do that. You've already screwed it up before." Over and over. I've been scolded, reprimanded and every other word you can think of to throw in there relating to punishment. But the reason I pressed on is I know there's a higher calling. I knew, when I had that dream in prison, there was something to it. That I had to make it happen. I knew I had to deliver books, trainings, videos and everything else, in order to spread my message. I couldn't just leave it lying dormant. We all have a story in us. We all have amesomeness we can deliver. The problem is we all have that one person (or maybe more) in our life who's telling us we shouldn't do it.

For years, I wanted to tell this story and write this book, but I was concerned with how my parents might feel about it. I was concerned with how my ex-wives might feel about it. I'm not concerned anymore because I have a message. Whatever comes my way, will come my way. I'm willing to fight on because the mindset I have is that there is a message I have to deliver to this marketplace, to people struggling everywhere. If it means being criticized, suffering lawsuits, or whatever the case may be, it doesn't matter, I still have a message to deliver. I'm willing to bear that burden in order to show you there's somebody out here who overcame the odds and is making shit happen. You need to adopt that same mindset as well. If you're going to survive in this cold world where everything is trying to kill you, you have to understand what it's like to be on guard. Be intentional with everything you do. One of the keys to being a closer is being intentional.

"Intentional." It's a really simple word. Everybody knows what it means, but very few people actually implement it. Most people arrive on sales calls, or job interviews, or whatever the case may be, with no endgame other than, "Well, you know, hopefully, they buy my shit." A closer arrives with the mindset of intent. On top of confidence, this is the most powerful thing you can do, because the average person doesn't have intent. When you are selling your product, when you are closing that person, they have no idea you have intent because they don't have it, and it's foreign to them. However, if you go into a sales call, you need to have an intention. That intention is to get a confession out of them, to make a sale and close the transaction. When you have a specific process you've put together in order to accomplish the end goal, that's when you're able to operate from the perspective of a closer. It takes a mindset of determination and a mindset of intention to be able to do that.

I'm going to share with you my step-by-step sales process I've put together over the years based on my different experiences as a sales person and all the transactions I've closed, the money I've made, what I've learned from my mentors and the people around me. In order to have intention, you must have a game plan. We have business plans, but we have no sales plan. We just know the end result is, "Hopefully, I can convince them, somehow, to give me some money for what I have."

Let me show you a way to arrive at a powerful sales conversation that will change the game on how you're able to close people and communicate with people, especially in today's social media world. If someone comes to you, or if you're prospecting on social media, and you're aggressive, or pushy, or annoying, they will unfriend you, block you and then talk behind your back to their other friends about why they wouldn't buy your shit and how fucking weird you are. You've got to know how to operate without being douchey and without being so aggressive it scares people off. You have to do this, yet at the same time, be bold enough to say what needs to be said to close the sale. It works like this. I call it "The Closer." Here's how the acronym works.

The "C" in closer stands for "Clarify why they are there." "There" could be on a phone call with you. "There" could be on a private chat message with you. "There" might mean a back-and-forth email exchange. One of the biggest mistakes salespeople make is when someone is chatting with you, your potential client starts thinking about buying your stuff and giving you money on Facebook, and the salesperson tries to get them on the phone. If a salesperson is on the phone with them, then they will try to get the prospect to email them details. People avoid direct decisions. They will try to put more barriers between you. It works both ways. The clients or prospects will avoid it. The salespeople will do the same thing, too, because it's a mentality. "I'm good here. So, I need to close them here." No. What you need to do is get good everywhere. If you're good on the phone and face-to-face, but suck at email, then work on your writing skills. I highly recommend buying a copy of John Carlton's *Kick-Ass Copywriting Secrets of a Marketing Rebel*. Great book. Pick it up. Learn to write.

People like to watch videos, so learn to sell via video. Obviously, it works.

Commercials air every 13 minutes or less on every TV channel out there. Some TV channels blast all day, 24/7 commercials. That ought to tell you something.

Simply ask your prospect, "What made you decide to reach out to me?" It's a very powerful phrase. Let me explain the mentality behind it. When you ask your customer, "What made you decide to reach out to me?" and they answer, they're giving you a subconscious neurological confession centered on making their decision. By simply answering your question, they have admitted to you they have already made a decision. Coaxing a human being to make a decision is one of the hardest actions you can get them to take on earth, especially with so many different choices at our disposal right now. When they answer, you will have accomplished one of the toughest things on this planet that has to do with another human. And you will have done it all in one sentence by phrasing your question in such a way that they have no choice but to give you an answer. If you deviate from this plan, it will not work. You have to use this exact phrase, "What made you decide to reach out to me?"

Power exists in words. What's going to happen is that client's going to tell you, "Well, you know, I saw your post on Facebook," or, "Well, I saw your advertisement in a magazine," or "I saw this, that and the other. I was thinking maybe you can help me." The natural tendency of a salesperson is to respond, "Awesome. It's X, Y, Z money for me to help you. I can do this, this, this, this, this." That's so wrong. That's the exact wrong way to present yourself. Remember "C": "Clarify why your prospect is there." Ask them, "Hey, what made you decide to reach out to me?" They are going to give you their answer and the next letter in the acronym, "L" stands for "Let them know how the call works."

Immediately after you inquire, "What made you decide to reach out to me?" and they give you their answer, say, "Awesome! What I would like to do is ask you a few questions and I would like you to answer them for me with complete honesty. While I am asking questions, if you don't understand anything or you have any questions, feel free to interrupt me and I will answer them for you as well. Does that sound cool?"

You've gotten them to shine their mind to your agenda. You have flipped around the whole sales process. You have already gotten them to make a decision to reach out to you and say they need you. Second of all, you have to let them know the agenda. So, instead of pouncing on them like every other salesperson has done in their entire life, you are mellow like, "Tell me about your situation."

That's when you "O." You "Open up the dialogue with questions." They have now told you why they are there with you:

because they're looking for information or have a question about your businesses. Your job is not to talk about your business. Your job is to talk about their business and their problems. Your job is to ask questions until you can find out exactly what it is they are there for.

I have given you the example from back when I trained real estate agents. They would show up on a phone call and I knew from the beginning of the call, because I was so in touch with my audience and every real estate agent that got on the phone with me, that they wanted one or two things. They wanted more leads because they did not have enough work, or they wanted more time off because they had too much work. There was no in-between. Everybody who picked up the call from me had a perfect audience. For your perfect customer, their root need is to have an ideal audience.

My job, when I arrive on the scene to call, is to get the client to make a decision. I let them know why they are there and the agenda. Then I open up with questions, poking them with things like, "So tell me about your business. You working really hard right now?" or "Do you wish you had more stuff to do?" Because I have intention. I know exactly where I am leading them. I am getting them to confess one or two wants to me ultimately. Once they confess, we move on to "S."

"You, Jason have to make a decision," I say. Because Jason has said, "The reason I am here is because I have so much business I don't know what to do. I hate the team members that are working for me. I can't get people to pay attention to what I am saying. I am working on Saturdays and I'd really rather be at my kid's soccer game."

My reply, as I move into the next phase: "S," which stands for "Solve their problem," would be, "That's awesome, it sounds like you need auto-responders and videos in a social media posting strategy, where you can be out and about without a problem and still communicate with people without them knowing that you are not communicating with them. We can set all that up for you. The price will be $10,500. And I can finance that over 90 days, or I can actually give you a thousand dollars off the price, making it $9,500 if you pay it in full, but I know it's up to you."

Now I have incentivized them. I have given them an incentive to make a decision and I have engaged them in making a decision. That's right I have moved on to "E," "Engage your client to make a decision." I have basically extended the offer.

Finally, I apply "R," "Relentless and repeated follow up," whether they buy or not. If they don't buy, because maybe they don't have the money, or for whatever reason, I will circle around. If they turn me down, that's awesome. My favorite thing to do is give them a few videos from my blog for free and leave them with, "Thanks for reaching out. I think you will enjoy these videos after our talk. They are most applicable to your situation. If things change in the future, feel free to reach out to me." Then I continue posting on Facebook on a regular basis. I'm still their friend. If I go on to rub the success in their face long enough, they are going to come back and give me another shot, especially if they like the videos I gave them. It's super special if they make some money from the videos I gave them. It's about "Relentless and repeated follow ups."

Let me go over this again.

C- Clarify. Why they are there? *What's one thing that made you decide to reach out to me?*

L- Let them know how the call works. Get them on an agenda. I am going to ask some questions; give me answers. Meanwhile, if you have any questions for me, I will give you the answers. *Are we cool with that*?

O-Open up dialogue. Ask them the questions. Go in with tips.

S-Solve their problem. Show them what you have to fix their problem.

E-Engage them into a decision. Make them an offer.

R-Relentlessly and repeatedly follow up with them.

You see when you go into a sales conversation with that mindset and with that intention, you are stepping into a whole new realm. It's an entirely different operational side of the closing business. You see so many people talking about how cool things are and using all these buzzwords and fancy graphics. Meanwhile, you are trying to find out what somebody's real problem is and how you can potentially solve that problem and get paid in exchange for it. It's a beautiful thing.

Let's talk about sales. Let's talk about the sides nobody ever talks about. If you are in the business of selling stuff and if you're reading this, then you have to understand that sales start at the first impression. Many times these days, that person's first impression is on social media. It could be Facebook; it could be YouTube. It could be an email they see somewhere. But many times that first impression is online and they have only a couple of seconds to either click or read further, or reject you or whatever the case may be, regardless selling starts at that first impression.

I said earlier you've got to understand how to sell words, spoken and written. That includes video, audio, chat, email and everything in between. You have got to learn to sell any way you can face-to-face. You are not a true master salesperson until you have conquered all areas. You are not a true master salesperson until you can effectively close on video, with your written word, and until you can effectively close back and forth through your email. Then you don't have to deter somebody from a Facebook chat to a phone call because you are master of closing a Facebook chat. On your videos, when you close somebody and tell them to hit the link and pay, they do it.

That is what makes you a Closer. Very few people buy on the first impression. We know an average buyer looks at a product 8 to12 times before they buy. The days of impulse buys are still here, but for big tickets, it's your job to brand yourself, to make those first impressions and then to continue to make impressions after that. If it takes 8 to12 touches to bite, think about mail or email. You can't hit somebody 8 to 12 times in the daily mail. They just throw your stuff away and think it was a mistake. If you sent 8 to 12 emails out over the same number of days, somebody will probably unsubscribe from your list. Here's the cool part. On social media and through the Internet, we have the ability to use different mediums and different lines of connection to still hit our 8 to 12 familiarity points. Before, you would have to send eight letters out per week through mail or email. Or you would have to make eight phone calls or eight cold calls, to become familiar. Now, thanks to Facebook, you can like their status. They see your name. It's brand new. You could comment on their status, and get them to comment back. That's a couple of times they've seen your name. They could see your post in the news feed and all of a sudden because your affinity is up in your EdgeRank, then, you score a fourth time that they've seen your name. They could comment on your status or like it, and that might be the fifth or sixth time they have seen your name, all within a couple of minutes. Then, they scroll through your wall to get to know who you are a little bit better. Maybe that's the seventh or eighth time. They could hit a couple of like buttons. The next day, you could follow up with them. Maybe they checked their inbox, and realized that you've also sent them an email with a video attached to it.

What would normally take months, or at the bare minimum, weeks to brand yourself, you're now able to do in far less time thanks to social media and the Internet and you can do it without it seeming like you just bombarded somebody eight days in a row with emails. You sent them one email, liked a couple of their Facebook posts, and maybe left a comment on their LinkedIn profile. Spread it out.

You could remark, "Well, that's creeperish." No, that's letting somebody know that you paid attention to them. If they're a good prospect, they'll like to know they are receiving attention. That's why people are on social media and why they post on Facebook—so someone will acknowledge their thoughts and feelings. It's your job to oblige them, especially people that have fan pages. Fan pages, these days, on Facebook get minimal engagement unless you pay, or unless there's some kind of viral fan page, which most don't have.

The friend request on Facebook is familiarity point number one. The acceptance is familiarity point number two. Then you can write on their wall: familiarity point number three. They could like it and comment, that's four and five and so on and so forth.

The cool thing about fan pages is they don't usually get much engagement. You could comment on a post on a fan page or send a private message to a fan page. You can almost always bet that it's going to get read and replied to because people get excited, since nobody comments or writes on fan pages anymore. Even if you can't send them a friend request, but you can find their fan page, whoever it is, that's your prospect. You can start the closer process and the marketing and sales process right there, all from their fan page.

The best closers I know use seriously powerful questions. Questions like, "What made you decide to reach out to me?" They use power in every part of their process, but powerful questions are the most important part of the sales process. A salesman is not a tales man. A salesman is a salesman. They are someone who is supposed to sell a solution to somebody, not necessarily talk themselves into a sale.

My favorite button on the phone is the mute button because I can say whatever I want to, and I won't be able to interrupt and all that other shit. People don't like to be interrupted. People don't like to get sidetracked, railroaded and talked over. I just use the mute button. When the person is done, I go and make my points. The more the prospect talks, the more likely you are to close the deal. There's this Fear-O-Meter, if you could imagine a needle on an Applause-O-Meter, where it goes back and forth the higher the applause, then picture the Fear-O-Meter. When two people arrive into a sales conversation, fear is present on both sides. The salesman has a fear of "Oh shit, what if I blow the sale and don't get paid? I need this money." The prospect's fear sounds more like, "Oh, what? This dude is going to pressure me into buying something I don't want. I'm such a pussy." As that conversation is taking place, what's happened is that the Fear-O-Meter is going from prospect to salesman. Who's scared more? I tell you, the person who talks the most loses.

Be sure to ask open-ended questions. A guy from *60 Minutes* interviewed Elon Musk a few months ago. A reporter from

20/20 also interviewed him, so we compared the two interviews.

The guy from *60 Minutes*, asked questions like, "Well, Elon Musk, where do you see yourself in the future?" While the guy from *20/20*'s questions were along the lines of, "Elon Musk, where do you see yourself in the future? Is it with kids? Are you going to have a wife? Are you going to have safety cars, space cars? What do you see?"

Most people would think the guy that gave him several options would get the longer answer. The fact is the guy that asked him the shortest question left the most explaining to do on Elon's part. He had to talk more to cover the dead air because the guy didn't preload questions. Preloaded inquiries narrow your prospect's responses because all they have to do is say, "Yeah, the spaceship thing." It's your job to give your prospective client the room to talk.

Don't draw your prospects to their conclusions. Let them draw their own. "Yeah? So what made you decide to reach out to me?" Then you go through the process. When you get to open up the dialog with questions, you might say, "So how much money are you producing on a monthly basis now?" This is a question we ask often in my business. I let them answer, then say, "How much do you want to produce?" I let them answer, and then ask, "Well, why aren't you there?" I let them give me the answer. Then we work from there. The biggest takeaway is that *I let them talk*. There is a reason they are sharing their problems with me. They know they arrived on that call for a real reason, too. That's one my favorite phrases. "You're on this call for a real reason. You're here because something led you to get here. Let's get to that, see if I can help you solve it, and see if it's worth it to you for me to solve it." It all starts with powerful questions. Short, simple, to-the-point questions are the most powerful ones you can ask.

Let me share some powerful closes. You don't have to be super aggressive and pushy. You don't have to be mean to clients. You just have to be willing to correct them if they're not telling the right story. You have to be willing to ask them for the business. My favorite way to close the sale is to show somebody results in advance. I do this by telling them and explaining in great detail exactly what they could do to solve their problem. Then I ask them, "Hey, by the way, if you'd like help with that, it's what I do. It's $15,000 an hour or whatever the fee may be."

One very simple, very subtle question is, "Hey, by the way, if you would like help with that, that's something that I can take care of for $15,000 an hour. What do you think?" I'm going to let them offer it to me. They may say something like, "Well, that's a really hefty price." My best close formula, if I get a price objection, is to work the numbers with them. "OK, first, so it's going to cost you $15,000 for this hour, but in the next 48 hours, you will have made $60,000 from it. So I'd say that it's 500 percent on a rise. Not a bad gig for a guy."

Which reminds me of a story.

A guy goes to hang out with his buddy on the weekend. He bites into a beer bottle drunk, busts his tooth in. It's hanging from his mouth and bothering him. On Monday, the dentist's office opens up. He goes in and the doc pulls his tooth out in two seconds. Then he tells the guy, "That will be 600 bucks."

The guy says, "Wow, 600 bucks for like two seconds worth of work, man? That's a lot of money, don't you think?" The dentist snaps, "Well, I could have taken as long as you wanted, but I figured you'd want it removed immediately."

You have to think of that perspective. You have to think of that abundance mentality. When people give you a price rejection, you need to show them the value. When I first started selling mortgage mastermind spots it was $5,000 for 90 days. I had to show people that, "If we, over the course of three months, can't add two more loans to your pipeline at $150,000, two points each, so if we can't add $6,000, which is a thousand dollars above your investment in 90 days minimum, then we didn't do our job correctly."

Here's my favorite close. It's a very powerful close and it goes like this, "Hey, man, I hear your problem, and I can honestly solve it for you. I don't offer this to everybody, but I want you to understand this. I like you. I want to work with you, and I will go all-in with you. I will not let you fail. I will guarantee your success. I will get in the trenches for you. I will make phone calls for you, if I have to, to ensure that you are not let down and that you are successful. But you have to be willing to work, too. I'm willing to go toe-to-toe with you right now and get in the trenches. If you invest in me, I'll invest in you one- hundred percent. Let's go. What's it going to be?"

It's hard for anybody to say no to that. The thing is you have to be operating from a space of extreme confidence, extreme clarity and extreme commitment to make that offer. If you offer to go toe-to-toe with them, telling them that no man will be left behind, that you're going to guarantee their success and everything else…and then you don't do it…then fuck you. You are the problem with the sales industry. For those of us that can deliver on our word, who operate with integrity, and will go in there and deliver exactly what it is we promised our prospects we'll deliver, that's when the magic happens. Most people don't feel like somebody cares about them. When you're willing to care, to show you're committed to them, to go toe-to-toe with them, that you feel their pain, you're empathetic and you're ready to burst free and fight with them, they will catch that energy. They love it.

They trust you. But you cannot disobey and misuse your clients' trust because you get one shot. In these days of social media, if you make a bold promise and you don't deliver on it, you won't be able to close anybody else because they'll have that doubt in the back of their mind, and all a dissatisfied customer has to write is, "Hey, I hired this person. Don't hire him. Here's my experience."

I see posts on Facebook every day where people are complaining about how the services they got weren't right. These days, as soon as the company does wrong, what happens? The client sends them a tweet because they know the public can see tweets and companies respond to them to make it seem like they have the situation under control. It's faster than the 800 number.

The key to being a powerful closer is to have confidence. Nothing more, nothing less. Being 100 percent sure that you can absolutely solve the problem for your prospect. What happens with a lot of salespeople is we operate from a place of desperation. We have the attitude that we had to take this sales job, just selling anything, because we know we can sell, we just don't really believe in what we sell. Then, the people don't buy it and we end up in this fucking chain cycle of being broke, beaten and full of self-doubt, where we feel like, "Maybe I'm not a salesman after all. Maybe I thought I was, but maybe what I was selling before was just too easy, because I can't seem to sell this." No. What's happened is you don't believe in what you're selling. Never take a sales job out of desperation. Only sell something you would use yourself or actually do use yourself and whose value is worth five times more the price you pay.

As I'm writing this book right now, our masterminds programs range from $500 to $25,000. Our products range from free to $25,000 to $50,000, depending on what people want. I'm not going to try to push somebody that should be in a $27 product into a $50,000 product. It's not in me. I can't guarantee results on the $27 product, but I can give them an opportunity to learn and grow from it. When I make a claim to somebody, they know the goods will be delivered.

The guys that sell for me can tell you this is the best program. Hiring salespeople is a big deal in today's world, because there aren't very many good ones. The best way I've experienced to hire salespeople, is to hire those who've gone through my programs. They are the top-performers. Someone who's successfully completed my program and experienced it firsthand, is a person who is convicted. For example, Clayton Eason and Rob Sekel. Both have been paid clients and they sell for me at this point. They're convicted. When someone asks questions, I want them to talk about their experience. If that salesperson has been through the program, you're talking to someone who has experience. When they say, "I still pay to be in the group and I sell his stuff," that's a powerful close. Any time you can get a referral to sell your stuff for you, you're winning. We know that.

Let's wrap this book up. I told you a story of many failures. I told you a story of many struggles, but I didn't even tell you a third of the story. The crazy part is, they call me Hardcore Closer because of the lifestyle I've lived, not due to some pushy sales attitude. I can get that attitude, but these days I feel bad to really unleash the beast on people. When I find somebody who I believe wholeheartedly could 100 percent benefit from getting on board and that I could dramatically impact their life, I'll stop at nothing to make that happen. You can ask any of my clients.

I'm very selective, but I earned the ability to be this way. Being selective in choosing my clients means I only work with people I really like. It means only working with people that I would be friends with even if they didn't pay me and only helping people I would probably help for free if this wasn't my job. I've been able to design that. All the people who judge me for being a felon, smoking weed, or having past drug issues, those people aren't around anymore. I've cleansed them. They're not around on Facebook. They're not around ever.

I've worked with celebrities, from Fredrik Eklund, Josh Flagg, Josh Altman, Dan Bilzerian, and Ronnie Coleman. I've worked with athletes, trainers, authors, coaches and speakers. Never once have my multiple felonies gotten in the way. As a matter of fact, the only time somebody ever asked about my felonies, it was, "So what'd you do? Tell me the story. What was it like in there?" I want you to understand, there are a lot of convicted felons in sales. A lot of us have to take sales jobs because that's our only choice, and I want to say something to all of them in particular.

Don't fall back into crime. The shit doesn't pay. We typically don't buy drugs from somebody in a Lamborghini or a Bentley in a mansion. We typically buy drugs from somebody that's more busted than we are. We see drug dealers on TV living lavish lifestyles, but they're few and far between. There are so many more people failing to win. So don't fall back on that. Stay true to yourself, okay? But find something you like. Find something you can use and go show your company with absolute conviction that you will work for them and dominate it, and they will take a chance on you. I don't give a fuck who they are. I've seen guys get out of prison and go immediately to work for Wells Fargo, Bank of America, Citi, Chase. I've seen guys who have committed white collar crimes become finance managers of car dealerships. I've seen it all. Because they had conviction and talent.

You look at our political system right now. Some of our congressmen and a lot of our politicians are convicted felons. They owe back taxes just like anybody else that hit hard times. Their supporters made an exception because somebody thought they had talent so they backed them.

There's an exception out there for you. You just have to be the exception. You have to show up. You have to have a mindset of *fuck anything that has come against me*. Whether I have been beaten, broke, robbed, imprisoned, adopted, bankrupt and divorced, it doesn't matter. You have to keep pushing towards your goal. Different things come at you and you have to deal with them. When life throws obstacles in your way, it's a good idea to be in shape so you can dodge them. You committed a crime, your parents gave up on you, you failed in business, your wife or husband left you or cheated on you, whatever the case may be. That doesn't mean it's over. It means you have to fight twice as hard. If you're going to kick ass and take names, emails and phone numbers, whether it be from girls you're trying to pick up at the bar or from clients on the Internet, nobody's going to give you their contact information if you're a loser.

I encourage you to pick yourself up. Look in the mirror and tell yourself that all the things society, government, and everyone else has said about you is not true. Go out into the world with intent and conviction and close some fucking sales, will you?

65469751R00079

Made in the USA
Lexington, KY
13 July 2017